Squash Workout and Nutrition Journal

This Book Belongs To:

_____

©Red Tiger Press

DATE:	WEEK:	WEIGHT:

Warm Up/ Stretching   **Duration:**

Exercise		Set 1	Set 2	Set 3	Set 4	Set 5
	Weight					
	Reps					
	Weight					
	Reps					
	Weight					
	Reps					
	Weight					
	Reps					
	Weight					
	Reps					
	Weight					
	Reps					
	Weight					
	Reps					
	Weight					
	Reps					
	Weight					
	Reps					
	Weight					
	Reps					
	Weight					
	Reps					
	Weight					
	Reps					
	Weight					
	Reps					

CARDIO WORKOUT

Exercise	Duration	Pace	Heart Rate	Calories

Notes:

DAILY CALORIE TARGET:

BREAKFAST	Protein	Carbs	Fat	Fiber	Sodium	Calories

SNACK	Protein	Carbs	Fat	Fiber	Sodium	Calories

LUNCH	Protein	Carbs	Fat	Fiber	Sodium	Calories

SNACK	Protein	Carbs	Fat	Fiber	Sodium	Calories

DINNER	Protein	Carbs	Fat	Fiber	Sodium	Calories

SNACK	Protein	Carbs	Fat	Fiber	Sodium	Calories

DAILY TOTALS						
DAILY GOALS						
% DAILY GOALS	%	%	%	%	%	%

WATER   1 cup per circle
(1 cup = 8 ounces ~ 240ml)   ○○○○○○○○○○○○○○

DATE:　　　　　　**WEEK:**　　　　**WEIGHT:**

Warm Up/ Stretching　　　　　　　　**Duration:**

Exercise		Set 1	Set 2	Set 3	Set 4	Set 5
	Weight					
	Reps					
	Weight					
	Reps					
	Weight					
	Reps					
	Weight					
	Reps					
	Weight					
	Reps					
	Weight					
	Reps					
	Weight					
	Reps					
	Weight					
	Reps					
	Weight					
	Reps					
	Weight					
	Reps					
	Weight					
	Reps					
	Weight					
	Reps					
	Weight					
	Reps					

CARDIO WORKOUT

Exercise	Duration	Pace	Heart Rate	Calories

Notes:

DAILY CALORIE TARGET:

BREAKFAST	Protein	Carbs	Fat	Fiber	Sodium	Calories

SNACK	Protein	Carbs	Fat	Fiber	Sodium	Calories

LUNCH	Protein	Carbs	Fat	Fiber	Sodium	Calories

SNACK	Protein	Carbs	Fat	Fiber	Sodium	Calories

DINNER	Protein	Carbs	Fat	Fiber	Sodium	Calories

SNACK	Protein	Carbs	Fat	Fiber	Sodium	Calories

	Protein	Carbs	Fat	Fiber	Sodium	Calories
DAILY TOTALS						
DAILY GOALS						
% DAILY GOALS	%	%	%	%	%	%

WATER   1 cup per circle
(1 cup = 8 ounces ~ 240ml)   ○ ○ ○ ○ ○ ○ ○ ○ ○ ○ ○ ○

DATE: **WEEK:**   **WEIGHT:**

Warm Up/ Stretching   **Duration:**

Exercise		Set 1	Set 2	Set 3	Set 4	Set 5
	Weight					
	Reps					
	Weight					
	Reps					
	Weight					
	Reps					
	Weight					
	Reps					
	Weight					
	Reps					
	Weight					
	Reps					
	Weight					
	Reps					
	Weight					
	Reps					
	Weight					
	Reps					
	Weight					
	Reps					
	Weight					
	Reps					
	Weight					
	Reps					

CARDIO WORKOUT

Exercise	Duration	Pace	Heart Rate	Calories

Notes:

DAILY CALORIE TARGET:

BREAKFAST	Protein	Carbs	Fat	Fiber	Sodium	Calories

SNACK	Protein	Carbs	Fat	Fiber	Sodium	Calories

LUNCH	Protein	Carbs	Fat	Fiber	Sodium	Calories

SNACK	Protein	Carbs	Fat	Fiber	Sodium	Calories

DINNER	Protein	Carbs	Fat	Fiber	Sodium	Calories

SNACK	Protein	Carbs	Fat	Fiber	Sodium	Calories

DAILY TOTALS						
DAILY GOALS						
% DAILY GOALS	%	%	%	%	%	%

WATER 1 cup per circle
(1 cup = 8 ounces ~ 240ml)   ○ ○ ○ ○ ○ ○ ○ ○ ○ ○ ○ ○

DATE: **WEEK:**   **WEIGHT:**

Warm Up/ Stretching   **Duration:**

Exercise		Set 1	Set 2	Set 3	Set 4	Set 5
	Weight					
	Reps					
	Weight					
	Reps					
	Weight					
	Reps					
	Weight					
	Reps					
	Weight					
	Reps					
	Weight					
	Reps					
	Weight					
	Reps					
	Weight					
	Reps					
	Weight					
	Reps					
	Weight					
	Reps					
	Weight					
	Reps					
	Weight					
	Reps					
	Weight					
	Reps					

CARDIO WORKOUT

Exercise	Duration	Pace	Heart Rate	Calories

Notes:

DAILY CALORIE TARGET: ☐

BREAKFAST	Protein	Carbs	Fat	Fiber	Sodium	Calories
SNACK	**Protein**	**Carbs**	**Fat**	**Fiber**	**Sodium**	**Calories**
LUNCH	**Protein**	**Carbs**	**Fat**	**Fiber**	**Sodium**	**Calories**
SNACK	**Protein**	**Carbs**	**Fat**	**Fiber**	**Sodium**	**Calories**
DINNER	**Protein**	**Carbs**	**Fat**	**Fiber**	**Sodium**	**Calories**
SNACK	**Protein**	**Carbs**	**Fat**	**Fiber**	**Sodium**	**Calories**
DAILY TOTALS						
DAILY GOALS						
% DAILY GOALS	%	%	%	%	%	%

WATER 1 cup per circle
(1 cup = 8 ounces ~ 240ml)   ○○○○○○○○○○○○

DATE: **WEEK:**   **WEIGHT:**

Warm Up/ Stretching

Duration:

Exercise		Set 1	Set 2	Set 3	Set 4	Set 5
	Weight					
	Reps					
	Weight					
	Reps					
	Weight					
	Reps					
	Weight					
	Reps					
	Weight					
	Reps					
	Weight					
	Reps					
	Weight					
	Reps					
	Weight					
	Reps					
	Weight					
	Reps					
	Weight					
	Reps					
	Weight					
	Reps					
	Weight					
	Reps					
	Weight					
	Reps					

CARDIO WORKOUT

Exercise	Duration	Pace	Heart Rate	Calories

Notes:

DAILY CALORIE TARGET:

BREAKFAST	Protein	Carbs	Fat	Fiber	Sodium	Calories

SNACK	Protein	Carbs	Fat	Fiber	Sodium	Calories

LUNCH	Protein	Carbs	Fat	Fiber	Sodium	Calories

SNACK	Protein	Carbs	Fat	Fiber	Sodium	Calories

DINNER	Protein	Carbs	Fat	Fiber	Sodium	Calories

SNACK	Protein	Carbs	Fat	Fiber	Sodium	Calories

DAILY TOTALS						
DAILY GOALS						
% DAILY GOALS	%	%	%	%	%	%

WATER 1 cup per circle
(1 cup = 8 ounces ~ 240ml)   ○○○○○○○○○○○○○○

DATE:	WEEK:	WEIGHT:

Warm Up/ Stretching

Duration:

Exercise		Set 1	Set 2	Set 3	Set 4	Set 5
	Weight					
	Reps					
	Weight					
	Reps					
	Weight					
	Reps					
	Weight					
	Reps					
	Weight					
	Reps					
	Weight					
	Reps					
	Weight					
	Reps					
	Weight					
	Reps					
	Weight					
	Reps					
	Weight					
	Reps					
	Weight					
	Reps					
	Weight					
	Reps					

CARDIO WORKOUT

Exercise	Duration	Pace	Heart Rate	Calories

Notes:

DAILY CALORIE TARGET: ☐

BREAKFAST	Protein	Carbs	Fat	Fiber	Sodium	Calories

SNACK	Protein	Carbs	Fat	Fiber	Sodium	Calories

LUNCH	Protein	Carbs	Fat	Fiber	Sodium	Calories

SNACK	Protein	Carbs	Fat	Fiber	Sodium	Calories

DINNER	Protein	Carbs	Fat	Fiber	Sodium	Calories

SNACK	Protein	Carbs	Fat	Fiber	Sodium	Calories

DAILY TOTALS						
DAILY GOALS						
% DAILY GOALS	%	%	%	%	%	%

WATER 1 cup per circle
(1 cup = 8 ounces ~ 240ml)   ○○○○○○○○○○○○○○○

DATE: **WEEK:** **WEIGHT:**

Warm Up/ Stretching **Duration:**

Exercise		Set 1	Set 2	Set 3	Set 4	Set 5
	Weight					
	Reps					
	Weight					
	Reps					
	Weight					
	Reps					
	Weight					
	Reps					
	Weight					
	Reps					
	Weight					
	Reps					
	Weight					
	Reps					
	Weight					
	Reps					
	Weight					
	Reps					
	Weight					
	Reps					
	Weight					
	Reps					
	Weight					
	Reps					

CARDIO WORKOUT

Exercise	Duration	Pace	Heart Rate	Calories

Notes:

DAILY CALORIE TARGET:

BREAKFAST	Protein	Carbs	Fat	Fiber	Sodium	Calories

SNACK	Protein	Carbs	Fat	Fiber	Sodium	Calories

LUNCH	Protein	Carbs	Fat	Fiber	Sodium	Calories

SNACK	Protein	Carbs	Fat	Fiber	Sodium	Calories

DINNER	Protein	Carbs	Fat	Fiber	Sodium	Calories

SNACK	Protein	Carbs	Fat	Fiber	Sodium	Calories

	Protein	Carbs	Fat	Fiber	Sodium	Calories
DAILY TOTALS						
DAILY GOALS						
% DAILY GOALS	%	%	%	%	%	%

WATER 1 cup per circle
(1 cup = 8 ounces ~ 240ml)   ○ ○ ○ ○ ○ ○ ○ ○ ○ ○ ○ ○ ○ ○

DATE:	WEEK:	WEIGHT:

Warm Up/ Stretching

Duration:

Exercise		Set 1	Set 2	Set 3	Set 4	Set 5
	Weight					
	Reps					
	Weight					
	Reps					
	Weight					
	Reps					
	Weight					
	Reps					
	Weight					
	Reps					
	Weight					
	Reps					
	Weight					
	Reps					
	Weight					
	Reps					
	Weight					
	Reps					
	Weight					
	Reps					
	Weight					
	Reps					
	Weight					
	Reps					
	Weight					
	Reps					

CARDIO WORKOUT

Exercise	Duration	Pace	Heart Rate	Calories

Notes:

DAILY CALORIE TARGET:

BREAKFAST	Protein	Carbs	Fat	Fiber	Sodium	Calories

SNACK	Protein	Carbs	Fat	Fiber	Sodium	Calories

LUNCH	Protein	Carbs	Fat	Fiber	Sodium	Calories

SNACK	Protein	Carbs	Fat	Fiber	Sodium	Calories

DINNER	Protein	Carbs	Fat	Fiber	Sodium	Calories

SNACK	Protein	Carbs	Fat	Fiber	Sodium	Calories
DAILY TOTALS						
DAILY GOALS						
% DAILY GOALS	%	%	%	%	%	%

WATER 1 cup per circle
(1 cup = 8 ounces ~ 240ml) ○○○○○○○○○○○○

DATE: **WEEK:** **WEIGHT:**

Warm Up/ Stretching **Duration:**

Exercise		Set 1	Set 2	Set 3	Set 4	Set 5
	Weight					
	Reps					
	Weight					
	Reps					
	Weight					
	Reps					
	Weight					
	Reps					
	Weight					
	Reps					
	Weight					
	Reps					
	Weight					
	Reps					
	Weight					
	Reps					
	Weight					
	Reps					
	Weight					
	Reps					
	Weight					
	Reps					
	Weight					
	Reps					
	Weight					
	Reps					

CARDIO WORKOUT

Exercise	Duration	Pace	Heart Rate	Calories

Notes:

DAILY CALORIE TARGET:

BREAKFAST	Protein	Carbs	Fat	Fiber	Sodium	Calories

SNACK	Protein	Carbs	Fat	Fiber	Sodium	Calories

LUNCH	Protein	Carbs	Fat	Fiber	Sodium	Calories

SNACK	Protein	Carbs	Fat	Fiber	Sodium	Calories

DINNER	Protein	Carbs	Fat	Fiber	Sodium	Calories

SNACK	Protein	Carbs	Fat	Fiber	Sodium	Calories

DAILY TOTALS						
DAILY GOALS						
% DAILY GOALS	%	%	%	%	%	%

WATER   1 cup per circle
(1 cup = 8 ounces ~ 240ml)   ○○○○○○○○○○○○○○

DATE: **WEEK:**   **WEIGHT:**

Warm Up/ Stretching   **Duration:**

Exercise		Set 1	Set 2	Set 3	Set 4	Set 5
	Weight					
	Reps					
	Weight					
	Reps					
	Weight					
	Reps					
	Weight					
	Reps					
	Weight					
	Reps					
	Weight					
	Reps					
	Weight					
	Reps					
	Weight					
	Reps					
	Weight					
	Reps					
	Weight					
	Reps					
	Weight					
	Reps					
	Weight					
	Reps					
	Weight					
	Reps					

CARDIO WORKOUT

Exercise	Duration	Pace	Heart Rate	Calories

Notes:

DAILY CALORIE TARGET:

BREAKFAST	Protein	Carbs	Fat	Fiber	Sodium	Calories

SNACK	Protein	Carbs	Fat	Fiber	Sodium	Calories

LUNCH	Protein	Carbs	Fat	Fiber	Sodium	Calories

SNACK	Protein	Carbs	Fat	Fiber	Sodium	Calories

DINNER	Protein	Carbs	Fat	Fiber	Sodium	Calories

SNACK	Protein	Carbs	Fat	Fiber	Sodium	Calories

	Protein	Carbs	Fat	Fiber	Sodium	Calories
DAILY TOTALS						
DAILY GOALS						
% DAILY GOALS	%	%	%	%	%	%

WATER   1 cup per circle
(1 cup = 8 ounces ~ 240ml)   ○○○○○○○○○○○○○○

| DATE: | | WEEK: | | WEIGHT: | |

Warm Up/ Stretching

Duration:

Exercise		Set 1	Set 2	Set 3	Set 4	Set 5
	Weight					
	Reps					
	Weight					
	Reps					
	Weight					
	Reps					
	Weight					
	Reps					
	Weight					
	Reps					
	Weight					
	Reps					
	Weight					
	Reps					
	Weight					
	Reps					
	Weight					
	Reps					
	Weight					
	Reps					
	Weight					
	Reps					
	Weight					
	Reps					
	Weight					
	Reps					

CARDIO WORKOUT

Exercise	Duration	Pace	Heart Rate	Calories

Notes:

DAILY CALORIE TARGET: [ ]

BREAKFAST	Protein	Carbs	Fat	Fiber	Sodium	Calories

SNACK	Protein	Carbs	Fat	Fiber	Sodium	Calories

LUNCH	Protein	Carbs	Fat	Fiber	Sodium	Calories

SNACK	Protein	Carbs	Fat	Fiber	Sodium	Calories

DINNER	Protein	Carbs	Fat	Fiber	Sodium	Calories

SNACK	Protein	Carbs	Fat	Fiber	Sodium	Calories

DAILY TOTALS						
DAILY GOALS						
% DAILY GOALS	%	%	%	%	%	%

WATER 1 cup per circle
(1 cup = 8 ounces ~ 240ml)

○○○○○○○○○○○○○○○○

DATE: □　　**WEEK:** □　　**WEIGHT:** □

Warm Up/ Stretching				Duration:	

Exercise		Set 1	Set 2	Set 3	Set 4	Set 5
	Weight					
	Reps					
	Weight					
	Reps					
	Weight					
	Reps					
	Weight					
	Reps					
	Weight					
	Reps					
	Weight					
	Reps					
	Weight					
	Reps					
	Weight					
	Reps					
	Weight					
	Reps					
	Weight					
	Reps					
	Weight					
	Reps					
	Weight					
	Reps					
	Weight					
	Reps					

CARDIO WORKOUT

Exercise	Duration	Pace	Heart Rate	Calories

Notes:

DAILY CALORIE TARGET:

BREAKFAST	Protein	Carbs	Fat	Fiber	Sodium	Calories

SNACK	Protein	Carbs	Fat	Fiber	Sodium	Calories

LUNCH	Protein	Carbs	Fat	Fiber	Sodium	Calories

SNACK	Protein	Carbs	Fat	Fiber	Sodium	Calories

DINNER	Protein	Carbs	Fat	Fiber	Sodium	Calories

SNACK	Protein	Carbs	Fat	Fiber	Sodium	Calories

	Protein	Carbs	Fat	Fiber	Sodium	Calories
DAILY TOTALS						
DAILY GOALS						
% DAILY GOALS	%	%	%	%	%	%

WATER 1 cup per circle
(1 cup = 8 ounces ~ 240ml)   ○ ○ ○ ○ ○ ○ ○ ○ ○ ○ ○ ○ ○ ○

DATE:		WEEK:		WEIGHT:	

Warm Up/ Stretching				Duration:	

Exercise		Set 1	Set 2	Set 3	Set 4	Set 5
	Weight					
	Reps					
	Weight					
	Reps					
	Weight					
	Reps					
	Weight					
	Reps					
	Weight					
	Reps					
	Weight					
	Reps					
	Weight					
	Reps					
	Weight					
	Reps					
	Weight					
	Reps					
	Weight					
	Reps					
	Weight					
	Reps					
	Weight					
	Reps					

CARDIO WORKOUT

Exercise	Duration	Pace	Heart Rate	Calories

Notes:

DAILY CALORIE TARGET: [ ]

BREAKFAST	Protein	Carbs	Fat	Fiber	Sodium	Calories

SNACK	Protein	Carbs	Fat	Fiber	Sodium	Calories

LUNCH	Protein	Carbs	Fat	Fiber	Sodium	Calories

SNACK	Protein	Carbs	Fat	Fiber	Sodium	Calories

DINNER	Protein	Carbs	Fat	Fiber	Sodium	Calories

SNACK	Protein	Carbs	Fat	Fiber	Sodium	Calories
DAILY TOTALS						
DAILY GOALS						
% DAILY GOALS	%	%	%	%	%	%

WATER 1 cup per circle
(1 cup = 8 ounces ~ 240ml)   ○○○○○○○○○○○○○○

| DATE: | | WEEK: | | WEIGHT: | |

| Warm Up/ Stretching | | | | Duration: | |

Exercise		Set 1	Set 2	Set 3	Set 4	Set 5
	Weight					
	Reps					
	Weight					
	Reps					
	Weight					
	Reps					
	Weight					
	Reps					
	Weight					
	Reps					
	Weight					
	Reps					
	Weight					
	Reps					
	Weight					
	Reps					
	Weight					
	Reps					
	Weight					
	Reps					
	Weight					
	Reps					
	Weight					
	Reps					
	Weight					
	Reps					

CARDIO WORKOUT

Exercise	Duration	Pace	Heart Rate	Calories

Notes:

DAILY CALORIE TARGET:

BREAKFAST	Protein	Carbs	Fat	Fiber	Sodium	Calories

SNACK	Protein	Carbs	Fat	Fiber	Sodium	Calories

LUNCH	Protein	Carbs	Fat	Fiber	Sodium	Calories

SNACK	Protein	Carbs	Fat	Fiber	Sodium	Calories

DINNER	Protein	Carbs	Fat	Fiber	Sodium	Calories

SNACK	Protein	Carbs	Fat	Fiber	Sodium	Calories
DAILY TOTALS						
DAILY GOALS						
% DAILY GOALS	%	%	%	%	%	%

WATER   1 cup per circle
(1 cup = 8 ounces ~ 240ml)

○ ○ ○ ○ ○ ○ ○ ○ ○ ○ ○ ○ ○ ○ ○

DATE:	WEEK:	WEIGHT:

Warm Up/ Stretching		Duration:				
Exercise		Set 1	Set 2	Set 3	Set 4	Set 5
	Weight					
	Reps					
	Weight					
	Reps					
	Weight					
	Reps					
	Weight					
	Reps					
	Weight					
	Reps					
	Weight					
	Reps					
	Weight					
	Reps					
	Weight					
	Reps					
	Weight					
	Reps					
	Weight					
	Reps					
	Weight					
	Reps					
	Weight					
	Reps					

CARDIO WORKOUT

Exercise	Duration	Pace	Heart Rate	Calories

Notes:

DAILY CALORIE TARGET:

BREAKFAST	Protein	Carbs	Fat	Fiber	Sodium	Calories

SNACK	Protein	Carbs	Fat	Fiber	Sodium	Calories

LUNCH	Protein	Carbs	Fat	Fiber	Sodium	Calories

SNACK	Protein	Carbs	Fat	Fiber	Sodium	Calories

DINNER	Protein	Carbs	Fat	Fiber	Sodium	Calories

SNACK	Protein	Carbs	Fat	Fiber	Sodium	Calories
DAILY TOTALS						
DAILY GOALS						
% DAILY GOALS	%	%	%	%	%	%

WATER   1 cup per circle
(1 cup = 8 ounces ~ 240ml)   ◯◯◯◯◯◯◯◯◯◯◯◯◯◯

DATE: **WEEK:** **WEIGHT:**

Warm Up/ Stretching					Duration:	
Exercise		Set 1	Set 2	Set 3	Set 4	Set 5
	Weight					
	Reps					
	Weight					
	Reps					
	Weight					
	Reps					
	Weight					
	Reps					
	Weight					
	Reps					
	Weight					
	Reps					
	Weight					
	Reps					
	Weight					
	Reps					
	Weight					
	Reps					
	Weight					
	Reps					
	Weight					
	Reps					
	Weight					
	Reps					

CARDIO WORKOUT

Exercise	Duration	Pace	Heart Rate	Calories

Notes:

DAILY CALORIE TARGET:

BREAKFAST	Protein	Carbs	Fat	Fiber	Sodium	Calories

SNACK	Protein	Carbs	Fat	Fiber	Sodium	Calories

LUNCH	Protein	Carbs	Fat	Fiber	Sodium	Calories

SNACK	Protein	Carbs	Fat	Fiber	Sodium	Calories

DINNER	Protein	Carbs	Fat	Fiber	Sodium	Calories

SNACK	Protein	Carbs	Fat	Fiber	Sodium	Calories

	Protein	Carbs	Fat	Fiber	Sodium	Calories
DAILY TOTALS						
DAILY GOALS						
% DAILY GOALS	%	%	%	%	%	%

WATER   1 cup per circle
(1 cup = 8 ounces ~ 240ml)   ○ ○ ○ ○ ○ ○ ○ ○ ○ ○ ○ ○

DATE: **WEEK:**   **WEIGHT:**

Warm Up/ Stretching   **Duration:**

Exercise		Set 1	Set 2	Set 3	Set 4	Set 5
	Weight					
	Reps					
	Weight					
	Reps					
	Weight					
	Reps					
	Weight					
	Reps					
	Weight					
	Reps					
	Weight					
	Reps					
	Weight					
	Reps					
	Weight					
	Reps					
	Weight					
	Reps					
	Weight					
	Reps					
	Weight					
	Reps					
	Weight					
	Reps					
	Weight					
	Reps					

CARDIO WORKOUT

Exercise	Duration	Pace	Heart Rate	Calories

Notes:

DAILY CALORIE TARGET:

BREAKFAST	Protein	Carbs	Fat	Fiber	Sodium	Calories

SNACK	Protein	Carbs	Fat	Fiber	Sodium	Calories

LUNCH	Protein	Carbs	Fat	Fiber	Sodium	Calories

SNACK	Protein	Carbs	Fat	Fiber	Sodium	Calories

DINNER	Protein	Carbs	Fat	Fiber	Sodium	Calories

SNACK	Protein	Carbs	Fat	Fiber	Sodium	Calories
DAILY TOTALS						
DAILY GOALS						
% DAILY GOALS	%	%	%	%	%	%

WATER   1 cup per circle
(1 cup = 8 ounces ~ 240ml)   ○○○○○○○○○○○○○○

DATE: **WEEK:** **WEIGHT:**

Warm Up/ Stretching
Duration:

Exercise		Set 1	Set 2	Set 3	Set 4	Set 5
	Weight					
	Reps					
	Weight					
	Reps					
	Weight					
	Reps					
	Weight					
	Reps					
	Weight					
	Reps					
	Weight					
	Reps					
	Weight					
	Reps					
	Weight					
	Reps					
	Weight					
	Reps					
	Weight					
	Reps					
	Weight					
	Reps					
	Weight					
	Reps					
	Weight					
	Reps					

CARDIO WORKOUT

Exercise	Duration	Pace	Heart Rate	Calories

Notes:

DAILY CALORIE TARGET:

BREAKFAST	Protein	Carbs	Fat	Fiber	Sodium	Calories

SNACK	Protein	Carbs	Fat	Fiber	Sodium	Calories

LUNCH	Protein	Carbs	Fat	Fiber	Sodium	Calories

SNACK	Protein	Carbs	Fat	Fiber	Sodium	Calories

DINNER	Protein	Carbs	Fat	Fiber	Sodium	Calories

SNACK	Protein	Carbs	Fat	Fiber	Sodium	Calories

DAILY TOTALS						
DAILY GOALS						
% DAILY GOALS	%	%	%	%	%	%

WATER 1 cup per circle
(1 cup = 8 ounces ~ 240ml)   ○○○○○○○○○○○○○○

DATE:		WEEK:		WEIGHT:	

Warm Up/ Stretching

Duration:

Exercise		Set 1	Set 2	Set 3	Set 4	Set 5
	Weight					
	Reps					
	Weight					
	Reps					
	Weight					
	Reps					
	Weight					
	Reps					
	Weight					
	Reps					
	Weight					
	Reps					
	Weight					
	Reps					
	Weight					
	Reps					
	Weight					
	Reps					
	Weight					
	Reps					
	Weight					
	Reps					
	Weight					
	Reps					

CARDIO WORKOUT

Exercise	Duration	Pace	Heart Rate	Calories

Notes:

DAILY CALORIE TARGET: ☐

BREAKFAST	Protein	Carbs	Fat	Fiber	Sodium	Calories

SNACK	Protein	Carbs	Fat	Fiber	Sodium	Calories

LUNCH	Protein	Carbs	Fat	Fiber	Sodium	Calories

SNACK	Protein	Carbs	Fat	Fiber	Sodium	Calories

DINNER	Protein	Carbs	Fat	Fiber	Sodium	Calories

SNACK	Protein	Carbs	Fat	Fiber	Sodium	Calories

DAILY TOTALS						
DAILY GOALS						
% DAILY GOALS	%	%	%	%	%	%

WATER   1 cup per circle
(1 cup = 8 ounces ~ 240ml)   ○○○○○○○○○○○○○○○

DATE: **WEEK:**   **WEIGHT:**

Warm Up/ Stretching   **Duration:**

Exercise		Set 1	Set 2	Set 3	Set 4	Set 5
	Weight					
	Reps					
	Weight					
	Reps					
	Weight					
	Reps					
	Weight					
	Reps					
	Weight					
	Reps					
	Weight					
	Reps					
	Weight					
	Reps					
	Weight					
	Reps					
	Weight					
	Reps					
	Weight					
	Reps					
	Weight					
	Reps					
	Weight					
	Reps					

CARDIO WORKOUT

Exercise	Duration	Pace	Heart Rate	Calories

Notes:

DAILY CALORIE TARGET: [ ]

BREAKFAST	Protein	Carbs	Fat	Fiber	Sodium	Calories
SNACK	**Protein**	**Carbs**	**Fat**	**Fiber**	**Sodium**	**Calories**
LUNCH	**Protein**	**Carbs**	**Fat**	**Fiber**	**Sodium**	**Calories**
SNACK	**Protein**	**Carbs**	**Fat**	**Fiber**	**Sodium**	**Calories**
DINNER	**Protein**	**Carbs**	**Fat**	**Fiber**	**Sodium**	**Calories**
SNACK	**Protein**	**Carbs**	**Fat**	**Fiber**	**Sodium**	**Calories**
DAILY TOTALS						
DAILY GOALS						
% DAILY GOALS	%	%	%	%	%	%

WATER   1 cup per circle
(1 cup = 8 ounces ~ 240ml)   ○ ○ ○ ○ ○ ○ ○ ○ ○ ○ ○ ○ ○ ○

DATE: **WEEK:** **WEIGHT:**

Warm Up/ Stretching **Duration:**

Exercise		Set 1	Set 2	Set 3	Set 4	Set 5
	Weight					
	Reps					
	Weight					
	Reps					
	Weight					
	Reps					
	Weight					
	Reps					
	Weight					
	Reps					
	Weight					
	Reps					
	Weight					
	Reps					
	Weight					
	Reps					
	Weight					
	Reps					
	Weight					
	Reps					
	Weight					
	Reps					
	Weight					
	Reps					

CARDIO WORKOUT

Exercise	Duration	Pace	Heart Rate	Calories

Notes:

DAILY CALORIE TARGET:

BREAKFAST	Protein	Carbs	Fat	Fiber	Sodium	Calories

SNACK	Protein	Carbs	Fat	Fiber	Sodium	Calories

LUNCH	Protein	Carbs	Fat	Fiber	Sodium	Calories

SNACK	Protein	Carbs	Fat	Fiber	Sodium	Calories

DINNER	Protein	Carbs	Fat	Fiber	Sodium	Calories

SNACK	Protein	Carbs	Fat	Fiber	Sodium	Calories

DAILY TOTALS						
DAILY GOALS						
% DAILY GOALS	%	%	%	%	%	%

WATER 1 cup per circle
(1 cup = 8 ounces ~ 240ml)

○○○○○○○○○○○○○○○

DATE:　　　　　　　**WEEK:**　　　　**WEIGHT:**

Warm Up/ Stretching　　　　　　　　　　　　Duration:

Exercise		Set 1	Set 2	Set 3	Set 4	Set 5
	Weight					
	Reps					
	Weight					
	Reps					
	Weight					
	Reps					
	Weight					
	Reps					
	Weight					
	Reps					
	Weight					
	Reps					
	Weight					
	Reps					
	Weight					
	Reps					
	Weight					
	Reps					
	Weight					
	Reps					
	Weight					
	Reps					
	Weight					
	Reps					

CARDIO WORKOUT

Exercise	Duration	Pace	Heart Rate	Calories

Notes:

DAILY CALORIE TARGET: [ ]

BREAKFAST	Protein	Carbs	Fat	Fiber	Sodium	Calories

SNACK	Protein	Carbs	Fat	Fiber	Sodium	Calories

LUNCH	Protein	Carbs	Fat	Fiber	Sodium	Calories

SNACK	Protein	Carbs	Fat	Fiber	Sodium	Calories

DINNER	Protein	Carbs	Fat	Fiber	Sodium	Calories

SNACK	Protein	Carbs	Fat	Fiber	Sodium	Calories

DAILY TOTALS						
DAILY GOALS						
% DAILY GOALS	%	%	%	%	%	%

WATER 1 cup per circle
(1 cup = 8 ounces ~ 240ml)   ○○○○○○○○○○○○○○

DATE: **WEEK:**   **WEIGHT:**

Warm Up/ Stretching   **Duration:**

Exercise		Set 1	Set 2	Set 3	Set 4	Set 5
	Weight					
	Reps					
	Weight					
	Reps					
	Weight					
	Reps					
	Weight					
	Reps					
	Weight					
	Reps					
	Weight					
	Reps					
	Weight					
	Reps					
	Weight					
	Reps					
	Weight					
	Reps					
	Weight					
	Reps					
	Weight					
	Reps					
	Weight					
	Reps					

CARDIO WORKOUT

Exercise	Duration	Pace	Heart Rate	Calories

Notes:

DAILY CALORIE TARGET:

BREAKFAST	Protein	Carbs	Fat	Fiber	Sodium	Calories

SNACK	Protein	Carbs	Fat	Fiber	Sodium	Calories

LUNCH	Protein	Carbs	Fat	Fiber	Sodium	Calories

SNACK	Protein	Carbs	Fat	Fiber	Sodium	Calories

DINNER	Protein	Carbs	Fat	Fiber	Sodium	Calories

SNACK	Protein	Carbs	Fat	Fiber	Sodium	Calories

DAILY TOTALS						
DAILY GOALS						
% DAILY GOALS	%	%	%	%	%	%

WATER   1 cup per circle
(1 cup = 8 ounces ~ 240ml)   ○○○○○○○○○○○○○○○

DATE: ⬚ **WEEK:** ⬚ **WEIGHT:** ⬚

Warm Up/ Stretching			Duration:			
Exercise		Set 1	Set 2	Set 3	Set 4	Set 5
	Weight					
	Reps					
	Weight					
	Reps					
	Weight					
	Reps					
	Weight					
	Reps					
	Weight					
	Reps					
	Weight					
	Reps					
	Weight					
	Reps					
	Weight					
	Reps					
	Weight					
	Reps					
	Weight					
	Reps					
	Weight					
	Reps					
	Weight					
	Reps					
	Weight					
	Reps					

CARDIO WORKOUT

Exercise	Duration	Pace	Heart Rate	Calories

Notes:

DAILY CALORIE TARGET: [ ]

BREAKFAST	Protein	Carbs	Fat	Fiber	Sodium	Calories
SNACK	Protein	Carbs	Fat	Fiber	Sodium	Calories
LUNCH	Protein	Carbs	Fat	Fiber	Sodium	Calories
SNACK	Protein	Carbs	Fat	Fiber	Sodium	Calories
DINNER	Protein	Carbs	Fat	Fiber	Sodium	Calories
SNACK	Protein	Carbs	Fat	Fiber	Sodium	Calories
DAILY TOTALS						
DAILY GOALS						
% DAILY GOALS	%	%	%	%	%	%

WATER 1 cup per circle
(1 cup = 8 ounces ~ 240ml)   ○ ○ ○ ○ ○ ○ ○ ○ ○ ○ ○ ○

| DATE: | | WEEK: | | WEIGHT: | |

| Warm Up/ Stretching | | | | Duration: | |

Exercise		Set 1	Set 2	Set 3	Set 4	Set 5
	Weight					
	Reps					
	Weight					
	Reps					
	Weight					
	Reps					
	Weight					
	Reps					
	Weight					
	Reps					
	Weight					
	Reps					
	Weight					
	Reps					
	Weight					
	Reps					
	Weight					
	Reps					
	Weight					
	Reps					
	Weight					
	Reps					
	Weight					
	Reps					
	Weight					
	Reps					

CARDIO WORKOUT

Exercise	Duration	Pace	Heart Rate	Calories

Notes:

DAILY CALORIE TARGET:

BREAKFAST	Protein	Carbs	Fat	Fiber	Sodium	Calories
SNACK	Protein	Carbs	Fat	Fiber	Sodium	Calories
LUNCH	Protein	Carbs	Fat	Fiber	Sodium	Calories
SNACK	Protein	Carbs	Fat	Fiber	Sodium	Calories
DINNER	Protein	Carbs	Fat	Fiber	Sodium	Calories
SNACK	Protein	Carbs	Fat	Fiber	Sodium	Calories
DAILY TOTALS						
DAILY GOALS						
% DAILY GOALS	%	%	%	%	%	%

WATER   1 cup per circle
(1 cup = 8 ounces ~ 240ml)   ○ ○ ○ ○ ○ ○ ○ ○ ○ ○ ○ ○

DATE: **WEEK:**   **WEIGHT:**

Warm Up/ Stretching   **Duration:**

Exercise		Set 1	Set 2	Set 3	Set 4	Set 5
	Weight					
	Reps					
	Weight					
	Reps					
	Weight					
	Reps					
	Weight					
	Reps					
	Weight					
	Reps					
	Weight					
	Reps					
	Weight					
	Reps					
	Weight					
	Reps					
	Weight					
	Reps					
	Weight					
	Reps					
	Weight					
	Reps					
	Weight					
	Reps					

CARDIO WORKOUT

Exercise	Duration	Pace	Heart Rate	Calories

Notes:

DAILY CALORIE TARGET:

BREAKFAST	Protein	Carbs	Fat	Fiber	Sodium	Calories

SNACK	Protein	Carbs	Fat	Fiber	Sodium	Calories

LUNCH	Protein	Carbs	Fat	Fiber	Sodium	Calories

SNACK	Protein	Carbs	Fat	Fiber	Sodium	Calories

DINNER	Protein	Carbs	Fat	Fiber	Sodium	Calories

SNACK	Protein	Carbs	Fat	Fiber	Sodium	Calories
DAILY TOTALS						
DAILY GOALS						
% DAILY GOALS	%	%	%	%	%	%

WATER   1 cup per circle
(1 cup = 8 ounces ~ 240ml)   ○○○○○○○○○○○○○○

DATE: **WEEK:** **WEIGHT:**

| Warm Up/ Stretching | | | | | | Duration: | |

Exercise		Set 1	Set 2	Set 3	Set 4	Set 5
	Weight					
	Reps					
	Weight					
	Reps					
	Weight					
	Reps					
	Weight					
	Reps					
	Weight					
	Reps					
	Weight					
	Reps					
	Weight					
	Reps					
	Weight					
	Reps					
	Weight					
	Reps					
	Weight					
	Reps					
	Weight					
	Reps					
	Weight					
	Reps					
	Weight					
	Reps					

CARDIO WORKOUT

Exercise	Duration	Pace	Heart Rate	Calories

Notes:

DAILY CALORIE TARGET: [ ]

BREAKFAST	Protein	Carbs	Fat	Fiber	Sodium	Calories

SNACK	Protein	Carbs	Fat	Fiber	Sodium	Calories

LUNCH	Protein	Carbs	Fat	Fiber	Sodium	Calories

SNACK	Protein	Carbs	Fat	Fiber	Sodium	Calories

DINNER	Protein	Carbs	Fat	Fiber	Sodium	Calories

SNACK	Protein	Carbs	Fat	Fiber	Sodium	Calories
DAILY TOTALS						
DAILY GOALS						
% DAILY GOALS	%	%	%	%	%	%

WATER   1 cup per circle
(1 cup = 8 ounces ~ 240ml)   ○○○○○○○○○○○○○○○

| DATE: | | WEEK: | | WEIGHT: | |

| Warm Up/ Stretching | | | | | Duration: | |

Exercise		Set 1	Set 2	Set 3	Set 4	Set 5
	Weight					
	Reps					
	Weight					
	Reps					
	Weight					
	Reps					
	Weight					
	Reps					
	Weight					
	Reps					
	Weight					
	Reps					
	Weight					
	Reps					
	Weight					
	Reps					
	Weight					
	Reps					
	Weight					
	Reps					
	Weight					
	Reps					
	Weight					
	Reps					
	Weight					
	Reps					

CARDIO WORKOUT

Exercise	Duration	Pace	Heart Rate	Calories

Notes:

DAILY CALORIE TARGET: [ ]

BREAKFAST	Protein	Carbs	Fat	Fiber	Sodium	Calories
SNACK	Protein	Carbs	Fat	Fiber	Sodium	Calories
LUNCH	Protein	Carbs	Fat	Fiber	Sodium	Calories
SNACK	Protein	Carbs	Fat	Fiber	Sodium	Calories
DINNER	Protein	Carbs	Fat	Fiber	Sodium	Calories
SNACK	Protein	Carbs	Fat	Fiber	Sodium	Calories
DAILY TOTALS						
DAILY GOALS						
% DAILY GOALS	%	%	%	%	%	%

WATER 1 cup per circle
(1 cup = 8 ounces ~ 240ml)   ○ ○ ○ ○ ○ ○ ○ ○ ○ ○ ○ ○

DATE:	WEEK:	WEIGHT:

Warm Up/ Stretching				Duration:		

Exercise		Set 1	Set 2	Set 3	Set 4	Set 5
	Weight					
	Reps					
	Weight					
	Reps					
	Weight					
	Reps					
	Weight					
	Reps					
	Weight					
	Reps					
	Weight					
	Reps					
	Weight					
	Reps					
	Weight					
	Reps					
	Weight					
	Reps					
	Weight					
	Reps					
	Weight					
	Reps					
	Weight					
	Reps					

CARDIO WORKOUT

Exercise	Duration	Pace	Heart Rate	Calories

Notes:

DAILY CALORIE TARGET:

BREAKFAST	Protein	Carbs	Fat	Fiber	Sodium	Calories

SNACK	Protein	Carbs	Fat	Fiber	Sodium	Calories

LUNCH	Protein	Carbs	Fat	Fiber	Sodium	Calories

SNACK	Protein	Carbs	Fat	Fiber	Sodium	Calories

DINNER	Protein	Carbs	Fat	Fiber	Sodium	Calories

SNACK	Protein	Carbs	Fat	Fiber	Sodium	Calories

DAILY TOTALS						
DAILY GOALS						
% DAILY GOALS	%	%	%	%	%	%

WATER   1 cup per circle
(1 cup = 8 ounces ~ 240ml)   ○○○○○○○○○○○○○○

DATE:	WEEK:	WEIGHT:

Warm Up/ Stretching

Duration:

Exercise		Set 1	Set 2	Set 3	Set 4	Set 5
	Weight					
	Reps					
	Weight					
	Reps					
	Weight					
	Reps					
	Weight					
	Reps					
	Weight					
	Reps					
	Weight					
	Reps					
	Weight					
	Reps					
	Weight					
	Reps					
	Weight					
	Reps					
	Weight					
	Reps					
	Weight					
	Reps					
	Weight					
	Reps					
	Weight					
	Reps					

CARDIO WORKOUT

Exercise	Duration	Pace	Heart Rate	Calories

Notes:

DAILY CALORIE TARGET:

BREAKFAST	Protein	Carbs	Fat	Fiber	Sodium	Calories

SNACK	Protein	Carbs	Fat	Fiber	Sodium	Calories

LUNCH	Protein	Carbs	Fat	Fiber	Sodium	Calories

SNACK	Protein	Carbs	Fat	Fiber	Sodium	Calories

DINNER	Protein	Carbs	Fat	Fiber	Sodium	Calories

SNACK	Protein	Carbs	Fat	Fiber	Sodium	Calories

	Protein	Carbs	Fat	Fiber	Sodium	Calories
DAILY TOTALS						
DAILY GOALS						
% DAILY GOALS	%	%	%	%	%	%

WATER 1 cup per circle
(1 cup = 8 ounces ~ 240ml)   ○ ○ ○ ○ ○ ○ ○ ○ ○ ○ ○ ○ ○ ○

DATE: **WEEK:** **WEIGHT:**

Warm Up/ Stretching **Duration:**

Exercise		Set 1	Set 2	Set 3	Set 4	Set 5
	Weight					
	Reps					
	Weight					
	Reps					
	Weight					
	Reps					
	Weight					
	Reps					
	Weight					
	Reps					
	Weight					
	Reps					
	Weight					
	Reps					
	Weight					
	Reps					
	Weight					
	Reps					
	Weight					
	Reps					
	Weight					
	Reps					
	Weight					
	Reps					
	Weight					
	Reps					

CARDIO WORKOUT

Exercise	Duration	Pace	Heart Rate	Calories

Notes:

DAILY CALORIE TARGET:

BREAKFAST	Protein	Carbs	Fat	Fiber	Sodium	Calories
SNACK	Protein	Carbs	Fat	Fiber	Sodium	Calories
LUNCH	Protein	Carbs	Fat	Fiber	Sodium	Calories
SNACK	Protein	Carbs	Fat	Fiber	Sodium	Calories
DINNER	Protein	Carbs	Fat	Fiber	Sodium	Calories
SNACK	Protein	Carbs	Fat	Fiber	Sodium	Calories
DAILY TOTALS						
DAILY GOALS						
% DAILY GOALS	%	%	%	%	%	%

WATER 1 cup per circle
(1 cup = 8 ounces ~ 240ml)   ○ ○ ○ ○ ○ ○ ○ ○ ○ ○ ○ ○ ○ ○

DATE:　　　　　　　　**WEEK:**　　　　**WEIGHT:**

Warm Up/ Stretching
Duration:

Exercise		Set 1	Set 2	Set 3	Set 4	Set 5
	Weight					
	Reps					
	Weight					
	Reps					
	Weight					
	Reps					
	Weight					
	Reps					
	Weight					
	Reps					
	Weight					
	Reps					
	Weight					
	Reps					
	Weight					
	Reps					
	Weight					
	Reps					
	Weight					
	Reps					
	Weight					
	Reps					
	Weight					
	Reps					

CARDIO WORKOUT

Exercise	Duration	Pace	Heart Rate	Calories

Notes:

DAILY CALORIE TARGET:

BREAKFAST	Protein	Carbs	Fat	Fiber	Sodium	Calories

SNACK	Protein	Carbs	Fat	Fiber	Sodium	Calories

LUNCH	Protein	Carbs	Fat	Fiber	Sodium	Calories

SNACK	Protein	Carbs	Fat	Fiber	Sodium	Calories

DINNER	Protein	Carbs	Fat	Fiber	Sodium	Calories

SNACK	Protein	Carbs	Fat	Fiber	Sodium	Calories

DAILY TOTALS						
DAILY GOALS						
% DAILY GOALS	%	%	%	%	%	%

WATER 1 cup per circle
(1 cup = 8 ounces ~ 240ml)   ◯◯◯◯◯◯◯◯◯◯◯◯◯◯

DATE: | **WEEK:** | **WEIGHT:**

Warm Up/ Stretching — **Duration:**

Exercise		Set 1	Set 2	Set 3	Set 4	Set 5
	Weight					
	Reps					
	Weight					
	Reps					
	Weight					
	Reps					
	Weight					
	Reps					
	Weight					
	Reps					
	Weight					
	Reps					
	Weight					
	Reps					
	Weight					
	Reps					
	Weight					
	Reps					
	Weight					
	Reps					
	Weight					
	Reps					
	Weight					
	Reps					

CARDIO WORKOUT

Exercise	Duration	Pace	Heart Rate	Calories

Notes:

DAILY CALORIE TARGET:

BREAKFAST	Protein	Carbs	Fat	Fiber	Sodium	Calories

SNACK	Protein	Carbs	Fat	Fiber	Sodium	Calories

LUNCH	Protein	Carbs	Fat	Fiber	Sodium	Calories

SNACK	Protein	Carbs	Fat	Fiber	Sodium	Calories

DINNER	Protein	Carbs	Fat	Fiber	Sodium	Calories

SNACK	Protein	Carbs	Fat	Fiber	Sodium	Calories

DAILY TOTALS						
DAILY GOALS						
% DAILY GOALS	%	%	%	%	%	%

WATER 1 cup per circle
(1 cup = 8 ounces ~ 240ml)   ○○○○○○○○○○○○○○

DATE:		WEEK:		WEIGHT:	

Warm Up/ Stretching				Duration:	

Exercise		Set 1	Set 2	Set 3	Set 4	Set 5
	Weight					
	Reps					
	Weight					
	Reps					
	Weight					
	Reps					
	Weight					
	Reps					
	Weight					
	Reps					
	Weight					
	Reps					
	Weight					
	Reps					
	Weight					
	Reps					
	Weight					
	Reps					
	Weight					
	Reps					
	Weight					
	Reps					
	Weight					
	Reps					

CARDIO WORKOUT

Exercise	Duration	Pace	Heart Rate	Calories

Notes:

DAILY CALORIE TARGET:

BREAKFAST	Protein	Carbs	Fat	Fiber	Sodium	Calories

SNACK	Protein	Carbs	Fat	Fiber	Sodium	Calories

LUNCH	Protein	Carbs	Fat	Fiber	Sodium	Calories

SNACK	Protein	Carbs	Fat	Fiber	Sodium	Calories

DINNER	Protein	Carbs	Fat	Fiber	Sodium	Calories

SNACK	Protein	Carbs	Fat	Fiber	Sodium	Calories

DAILY TOTALS						
DAILY GOALS						
% DAILY GOALS	%	%	%	%	%	%

WATER   1 cup per circle
(1 cup = 8 ounces ~ 240ml)   ○ ○ ○ ○ ○ ○ ○ ○ ○ ○ ○ ○

DATE: □ **WEEK:** □ **WEIGHT:** □

Warm Up/ Stretching **Duration:** □

Exercise		Set 1	Set 2	Set 3	Set 4	Set 5
	Weight					
	Reps					
	Weight					
	Reps					
	Weight					
	Reps					
	Weight					
	Reps					
	Weight					
	Reps					
	Weight					
	Reps					
	Weight					
	Reps					
	Weight					
	Reps					
	Weight					
	Reps					
	Weight					
	Reps					
	Weight					
	Reps					
	Weight					
	Reps					
	Weight					
	Reps					

CARDIO WORKOUT

Exercise	Duration	Pace	Heart Rate	Calories

Notes:

DAILY CALORIE TARGET:

BREAKFAST	Protein	Carbs	Fat	Fiber	Sodium	Calories
SNACK	Protein	Carbs	Fat	Fiber	Sodium	Calories
LUNCH	Protein	Carbs	Fat	Fiber	Sodium	Calories
SNACK	Protein	Carbs	Fat	Fiber	Sodium	Calories
DINNER	Protein	Carbs	Fat	Fiber	Sodium	Calories
SNACK	Protein	Carbs	Fat	Fiber	Sodium	Calories
DAILY TOTALS						
DAILY GOALS						
% DAILY GOALS	%	%	%	%	%	%

WATER   1 cup per circle
(1 cup = 8 ounces ~ 240ml)   ○○○○○○○○○○○○○○

DATE:	WEEK:	WEIGHT:

Warm Up/ Stretching		Duration:

Exercise		Set 1	Set 2	Set 3	Set 4	Set 5
	Weight					
	Reps					
	Weight					
	Reps					
	Weight					
	Reps					
	Weight					
	Reps					
	Weight					
	Reps					
	Weight					
	Reps					
	Weight					
	Reps					
	Weight					
	Reps					
	Weight					
	Reps					
	Weight					
	Reps					
	Weight					
	Reps					
	Weight					
	Reps					

CARDIO WORKOUT

Exercise	Duration	Pace	Heart Rate	Calories

Notes:

DAILY CALORIE TARGET:

BREAKFAST	Protein	Carbs	Fat	Fiber	Sodium	Calories

SNACK	Protein	Carbs	Fat	Fiber	Sodium	Calories

LUNCH	Protein	Carbs	Fat	Fiber	Sodium	Calories

SNACK	Protein	Carbs	Fat	Fiber	Sodium	Calories

DINNER	Protein	Carbs	Fat	Fiber	Sodium	Calories

SNACK	Protein	Carbs	Fat	Fiber	Sodium	Calories

DAILY TOTALS						
DAILY GOALS						
% DAILY GOALS	%	%	%	%	%	%

WATER 1 cup per circle
(1 cup = 8 ounces ~ 240ml)   ○ ○ ○ ○ ○ ○ ○ ○ ○ ○ ○ ○ ○ ○

DATE: [ ]   **WEEK:** [ ]   **WEIGHT:** [ ]

| Warm Up/ Stretching | | | | **Duration:** | |

Exercise		Set 1	Set 2	Set 3	Set 4	Set 5
	Weight					
	Reps					
	Weight					
	Reps					
	Weight					
	Reps					
	Weight					
	Reps					
	Weight					
	Reps					
	Weight					
	Reps					
	Weight					
	Reps					
	Weight					
	Reps					
	Weight					
	Reps					
	Weight					
	Reps					
	Weight					
	Reps					
	Weight					
	Reps					
	Weight					
	Reps					

CARDIO WORKOUT

Exercise	Duration	Pace	Heart Rate	Calories

Notes:

DAILY CALORIE TARGET:

BREAKFAST	Protein	Carbs	Fat	Fiber	Sodium	Calories

SNACK	Protein	Carbs	Fat	Fiber	Sodium	Calories

LUNCH	Protein	Carbs	Fat	Fiber	Sodium	Calories

SNACK	Protein	Carbs	Fat	Fiber	Sodium	Calories

DINNER	Protein	Carbs	Fat	Fiber	Sodium	Calories

SNACK	Protein	Carbs	Fat	Fiber	Sodium	Calories

DAILY TOTALS						
DAILY GOALS						
% DAILY GOALS	%	%	%	%	%	%

WATER 1 cup per circle
(1 cup = 8 ounces ~ 240ml)   ○○○○○○○○○○○○○

DATE: _____ **WEEK:** _____ **WEIGHT:** _____

Warm Up/ Stretching

Duration: _____

Exercise		Set 1	Set 2	Set 3	Set 4	Set 5
	Weight					
	Reps					
	Weight					
	Reps					
	Weight					
	Reps					
	Weight					
	Reps					
	Weight					
	Reps					
	Weight					
	Reps					
	Weight					
	Reps					
	Weight					
	Reps					
	Weight					
	Reps					
	Weight					
	Reps					
	Weight					
	Reps					
	Weight					
	Reps					
	Weight					
	Reps					

CARDIO WORKOUT

Exercise	Duration	Pace	Heart Rate	Calories

Notes:

DAILY CALORIE TARGET:

BREAKFAST	Protein	Carbs	Fat	Fiber	Sodium	Calories
SNACK	Protein	Carbs	Fat	Fiber	Sodium	Calories
LUNCH	Protein	Carbs	Fat	Fiber	Sodium	Calories
SNACK	Protein	Carbs	Fat	Fiber	Sodium	Calories
DINNER	Protein	Carbs	Fat	Fiber	Sodium	Calories
SNACK	Protein	Carbs	Fat	Fiber	Sodium	Calories
DAILY TOTALS						
DAILY GOALS						
% DAILY GOALS	%	%	%	%	%	%

WATER 1 cup per circle
(1 cup = 8 ounces ~ 240ml)   ○ ○ ○ ○ ○ ○ ○ ○ ○ ○ ○ ○ ○

DATE: **WEEK:** **WEIGHT:**

Warm Up/ Stretching **Duration:**

Exercise		Set 1	Set 2	Set 3	Set 4	Set 5
	Weight					
	Reps					
	Weight					
	Reps					
	Weight					
	Reps					
	Weight					
	Reps					
	Weight					
	Reps					
	Weight					
	Reps					
	Weight					
	Reps					
	Weight					
	Reps					
	Weight					
	Reps					
	Weight					
	Reps					
	Weight					
	Reps					
	Weight					
	Reps					
	Weight					
	Reps					

CARDIO WORKOUT

Exercise	Duration	Pace	Heart Rate	Calories

Notes:

DAILY CALORIE TARGET:

BREAKFAST	Protein	Carbs	Fat	Fiber	Sodium	Calories

SNACK	Protein	Carbs	Fat	Fiber	Sodium	Calories

LUNCH	Protein	Carbs	Fat	Fiber	Sodium	Calories

SNACK	Protein	Carbs	Fat	Fiber	Sodium	Calories

DINNER	Protein	Carbs	Fat	Fiber	Sodium	Calories

SNACK	Protein	Carbs	Fat	Fiber	Sodium	Calories

DAILY TOTALS						
DAILY GOALS						
% DAILY GOALS	%	%	%	%	%	%

WATER 1 cup per circle
(1 cup = 8 ounces ~ 240ml)   ○○○○○○○○○○○○○○

DATE: **WEEK:** **WEIGHT:**

| Warm Up/ Stretching | | | | **Duration:** | |

Exercise		Set 1	Set 2	Set 3	Set 4	Set 5
	Weight					
	Reps					
	Weight					
	Reps					
	Weight					
	Reps					
	Weight					
	Reps					
	Weight					
	Reps					
	Weight					
	Reps					
	Weight					
	Reps					
	Weight					
	Reps					
	Weight					
	Reps					
	Weight					
	Reps					
	Weight					
	Reps					
	Weight					
	Reps					

CARDIO WORKOUT

Exercise	Duration	Pace	Heart Rate	Calories

Notes:

DAILY CALORIE TARGET:

BREAKFAST		Protein	Carbs	Fat	Fiber	Sodium	Calories
SNACK		Protein	Carbs	Fat	Fiber	Sodium	Calories
LUNCH		Protein	Carbs	Fat	Fiber	Sodium	Calories
SNACK		Protein	Carbs	Fat	Fiber	Sodium	Calories
DINNER		Protein	Carbs	Fat	Fiber	Sodium	Calories
SNACK		Protein	Carbs	Fat	Fiber	Sodium	Calories
DAILY TOTALS							
DAILY GOALS							
% DAILY GOALS		%	%	%	%	%	%

WATER 1 cup per circle
(1 cup = 8 ounces ~ 240ml)

○ ○ ○ ○ ○ ○ ○ ○ ○ ○ ○ ○ ○ ○

DATE: | **WEEK:** | **WEIGHT:**

Warm Up/ Stretching

Duration:

Exercise		Set 1	Set 2	Set 3	Set 4	Set 5
	Weight					
	Reps					
	Weight					
	Reps					
	Weight					
	Reps					
	Weight					
	Reps					
	Weight					
	Reps					
	Weight					
	Reps					
	Weight					
	Reps					
	Weight					
	Reps					
	Weight					
	Reps					
	Weight					
	Reps					
	Weight					
	Reps					
	Weight					
	Reps					
	Weight					
	Reps					

CARDIO WORKOUT

Exercise	Duration	Pace	Heart Rate	Calories

Notes:

DAILY CALORIE TARGET:

BREAKFAST	Protein	Carbs	Fat	Fiber	Sodium	Calories

SNACK	Protein	Carbs	Fat	Fiber	Sodium	Calories

LUNCH	Protein	Carbs	Fat	Fiber	Sodium	Calories

SNACK	Protein	Carbs	Fat	Fiber	Sodium	Calories

DINNER	Protein	Carbs	Fat	Fiber	Sodium	Calories

SNACK	Protein	Carbs	Fat	Fiber	Sodium	Calories

DAILY TOTALS						
DAILY GOALS						
% DAILY GOALS	%	%	%	%	%	%

WATER 1 cup per circle
(1 cup = 8 ounces ~ 240ml)   ○ ○ ○ ○ ○ ○ ○ ○ ○ ○ ○ ○ ○ ○ ○

DATE: **WEEK:** **WEIGHT:**

Warm Up/ Stretching **Duration:**

Exercise		Set 1	Set 2	Set 3	Set 4	Set 5
	Weight					
	Reps					
	Weight					
	Reps					
	Weight					
	Reps					
	Weight					
	Reps					
	Weight					
	Reps					
	Weight					
	Reps					
	Weight					
	Reps					
	Weight					
	Reps					
	Weight					
	Reps					
	Weight					
	Reps					
	Weight					
	Reps					
	Weight					
	Reps					

CARDIO WORKOUT

Exercise	Duration	Pace	Heart Rate	Calories

Notes:

DAILY CALORIE TARGET:

BREAKFAST	Protein	Carbs	Fat	Fiber	Sodium	Calories
SNACK	Protein	Carbs	Fat	Fiber	Sodium	Calories
LUNCH	Protein	Carbs	Fat	Fiber	Sodium	Calories
SNACK	Protein	Carbs	Fat	Fiber	Sodium	Calories
DINNER	Protein	Carbs	Fat	Fiber	Sodium	Calories
SNACK	Protein	Carbs	Fat	Fiber	Sodium	Calories
DAILY TOTALS						
DAILY GOALS						
% DAILY GOALS	%	%	%	%	%	%

WATER 1 cup per circle
(1 cup = 8 ounces ~ 240ml)   ○ ○ ○ ○ ○ ○ ○ ○ ○ ○ ○ ○

DATE:	WEEK:	WEIGHT:

Warm Up/ Stretching — Duration:

Exercise		Set 1	Set 2	Set 3	Set 4	Set 5
	Weight					
	Reps					
	Weight					
	Reps					
	Weight					
	Reps					
	Weight					
	Reps					
	Weight					
	Reps					
	Weight					
	Reps					
	Weight					
	Reps					
	Weight					
	Reps					
	Weight					
	Reps					
	Weight					
	Reps					
	Weight					
	Reps					
	Weight					
	Reps					

CARDIO WORKOUT

Exercise	Duration	Pace	Heart Rate	Calories

Notes:

DAILY CALORIE TARGET:

BREAKFAST	Protein	Carbs	Fat	Fiber	Sodium	Calories
SNACK	Protein	Carbs	Fat	Fiber	Sodium	Calories
LUNCH	Protein	Carbs	Fat	Fiber	Sodium	Calories
SNACK	Protein	Carbs	Fat	Fiber	Sodium	Calories
DINNER	Protein	Carbs	Fat	Fiber	Sodium	Calories
SNACK	Protein	Carbs	Fat	Fiber	Sodium	Calories
DAILY TOTALS						
DAILY GOALS						
% DAILY GOALS	%	%	%	%	%	%

WATER 1 cup per circle
(1 cup = 8 ounces ~ 240ml)

○ ○ ○ ○ ○ ○ ○ ○ ○ ○ ○ ○ ○ ○ ○

DATE: _____   **WEEK:** _____   **WEIGHT:** _____

| Warm Up/ Stretching | | | | **Duration:** | |

Exercise		Set 1	Set 2	Set 3	Set 4	Set 5
	Weight					
	Reps					
	Weight					
	Reps					
	Weight					
	Reps					
	Weight					
	Reps					
	Weight					
	Reps					
	Weight					
	Reps					
	Weight					
	Reps					
	Weight					
	Reps					
	Weight					
	Reps					
	Weight					
	Reps					
	Weight					
	Reps					
	Weight					
	Reps					
	Weight					
	Reps					

CARDIO WORKOUT

Exercise	Duration	Pace	Heart Rate	Calories

Notes:

DAILY CALORIE TARGET:

BREAKFAST	Protein	Carbs	Fat	Fiber	Sodium	Calories

SNACK	Protein	Carbs	Fat	Fiber	Sodium	Calories

LUNCH	Protein	Carbs	Fat	Fiber	Sodium	Calories

SNACK	Protein	Carbs	Fat	Fiber	Sodium	Calories

DINNER	Protein	Carbs	Fat	Fiber	Sodium	Calories

SNACK	Protein	Carbs	Fat	Fiber	Sodium	Calories
DAILY TOTALS						
DAILY GOALS						
% DAILY GOALS	%	%	%	%	%	%

WATER 1 cup per circle
(1 cup = 8 ounces ~ 240ml)   ○○○○○○○○○○○○

DATE: **WEEK:**   **WEIGHT:**

Warm Up/ Stretching   **Duration:**

Exercise		Set 1	Set 2	Set 3	Set 4	Set 5
	Weight					
	Reps					
	Weight					
	Reps					
	Weight					
	Reps					
	Weight					
	Reps					
	Weight					
	Reps					
	Weight					
	Reps					
	Weight					
	Reps					
	Weight					
	Reps					
	Weight					
	Reps					
	Weight					
	Reps					
	Weight					
	Reps					
	Weight					
	Reps					

CARDIO WORKOUT

Exercise	Duration	Pace	Heart Rate	Calories

Notes:

DAILY CALORIE TARGET:

BREAKFAST	Protein	Carbs	Fat	Fiber	Sodium	Calories

SNACK	Protein	Carbs	Fat	Fiber	Sodium	Calories

LUNCH	Protein	Carbs	Fat	Fiber	Sodium	Calories

SNACK	Protein	Carbs	Fat	Fiber	Sodium	Calories

DINNER	Protein	Carbs	Fat	Fiber	Sodium	Calories

SNACK	Protein	Carbs	Fat	Fiber	Sodium	Calories

DAILY TOTALS						
DAILY GOALS						
% DAILY GOALS	%	%	%	%	%	%

WATER   1 cup per circle
(1 cup = 8 ounces ~ 240ml)

○ ○ ○ ○ ○ ○ ○ ○ ○ ○ ○ ○

DATE: WEEK: **WEIGHT:**

Warm Up/ Stretching **Duration:**

Exercise		Set 1	Set 2	Set 3	Set 4	Set 5
	Weight					
	Reps					
	Weight					
	Reps					
	Weight					
	Reps					
	Weight					
	Reps					
	Weight					
	Reps					
	Weight					
	Reps					
	Weight					
	Reps					
	Weight					
	Reps					
	Weight					
	Reps					
	Weight					
	Reps					
	Weight					
	Reps					
	Weight					
	Reps					
	Weight					
	Reps					

CARDIO WORKOUT

Exercise	Duration	Pace	Heart Rate	Calories

Notes:

DAILY CALORIE TARGET:

BREAKFAST	Protein	Carbs	Fat	Fiber	Sodium	Calories
SNACK	Protein	Carbs	Fat	Fiber	Sodium	Calories
LUNCH	Protein	Carbs	Fat	Fiber	Sodium	Calories
SNACK	Protein	Carbs	Fat	Fiber	Sodium	Calories
DINNER	Protein	Carbs	Fat	Fiber	Sodium	Calories
SNACK	Protein	Carbs	Fat	Fiber	Sodium	Calories
DAILY TOTALS						
DAILY GOALS						
% DAILY GOALS	%	%	%	%	%	%

WATER 1 cup per circle
(1 cup = 8 ounces ~ 240ml)

○ ○ ○ ○ ○ ○ ○ ○ ○ ○ ○ ○

DATE: _____ **WEEK:** _____ **WEIGHT:** _____

| Warm Up/ Stretching | | | **Duration:** | | |

Exercise		Set 1	Set 2	Set 3	Set 4	Set 5
	Weight					
	Reps					
	Weight					
	Reps					
	Weight					
	Reps					
	Weight					
	Reps					
	Weight					
	Reps					
	Weight					
	Reps					
	Weight					
	Reps					
	Weight					
	Reps					
	Weight					
	Reps					
	Weight					
	Reps					
	Weight					
	Reps					
	Weight					
	Reps					

CARDIO WORKOUT

Exercise	Duration	Pace	Heart Rate	Calories

Notes:

DAILY CALORIE TARGET:

BREAKFAST	Protein	Carbs	Fat	Fiber	Sodium	Calories

SNACK	Protein	Carbs	Fat	Fiber	Sodium	Calories

LUNCH	Protein	Carbs	Fat	Fiber	Sodium	Calories

SNACK	Protein	Carbs	Fat	Fiber	Sodium	Calories

DINNER	Protein	Carbs	Fat	Fiber	Sodium	Calories

SNACK	Protein	Carbs	Fat	Fiber	Sodium	Calories

DAILY TOTALS						
DAILY GOALS						
% DAILY GOALS	%	%	%	%	%	%

WATER   1 cup per circle
(1 cup = 8 ounces ~ 240ml)   ○ ○ ○ ○ ○ ○ ○ ○ ○ ○ ○ ○

DATE: WEEK: WEIGHT:

Warm Up/ Stretching Duration:

Exercise		Set 1	Set 2	Set 3	Set 4	Set 5
	Weight					
	Reps					
	Weight					
	Reps					
	Weight					
	Reps					
	Weight					
	Reps					
	Weight					
	Reps					
	Weight					
	Reps					
	Weight					
	Reps					
	Weight					
	Reps					
	Weight					
	Reps					
	Weight					
	Reps					
	Weight					
	Reps					
	Weight					
	Reps					

CARDIO WORKOUT

Exercise	Duration	Pace	Heart Rate	Calories

Notes:

DAILY CALORIE TARGET:

BREAKFAST	Protein	Carbs	Fat	Fiber	Sodium	Calories
SNACK	Protein	Carbs	Fat	Fiber	Sodium	Calories
LUNCH	Protein	Carbs	Fat	Fiber	Sodium	Calories
SNACK	Protein	Carbs	Fat	Fiber	Sodium	Calories
DINNER	Protein	Carbs	Fat	Fiber	Sodium	Calories
SNACK	Protein	Carbs	Fat	Fiber	Sodium	Calories
DAILY TOTALS						
DAILY GOALS						
% DAILY GOALS	%	%	%	%	%	%

WATER 1 cup per circle
(1 cup = 8 ounces ~ 240ml)   ○○○○○○○○○○○○

DATE: **WEEK:** **WEIGHT:**

| Warm Up/ Stretching | | | | | | **Duration:** | |

Exercise		Set 1	Set 2	Set 3	Set 4	Set 5
	Weight					
	Reps					
	Weight					
	Reps					
	Weight					
	Reps					
	Weight					
	Reps					
	Weight					
	Reps					
	Weight					
	Reps					
	Weight					
	Reps					
	Weight					
	Reps					
	Weight					
	Reps					
	Weight					
	Reps					
	Weight					
	Reps					
	Weight					
	Reps					
	Weight					
	Reps					

CARDIO WORKOUT

Exercise	Duration	Pace	Heart Rate	Calories

Notes:

DAILY CALORIE TARGET:

BREAKFAST	Protein	Carbs	Fat	Fiber	Sodium	Calories

SNACK	Protein	Carbs	Fat	Fiber	Sodium	Calories

LUNCH	Protein	Carbs	Fat	Fiber	Sodium	Calories

SNACK	Protein	Carbs	Fat	Fiber	Sodium	Calories

DINNER	Protein	Carbs	Fat	Fiber	Sodium	Calories

SNACK	Protein	Carbs	Fat	Fiber	Sodium	Calories

DAILY TOTALS						
DAILY GOALS						
% DAILY GOALS	%	%	%	%	%	%

WATER 1 cup per circle
(1 cup = 8 ounces ~ 240ml)   ○ ○ ○ ○ ○ ○ ○ ○ ○ ○ ○ ○ ○ ○

DATE: **WEEK:** **WEIGHT:**

| Warm Up/ Stretching | | | | | **Duration:** | |

Exercise		Set 1	Set 2	Set 3	Set 4	Set 5
	Weight					
	Reps					
	Weight					
	Reps					
	Weight					
	Reps					
	Weight					
	Reps					
	Weight					
	Reps					
	Weight					
	Reps					
	Weight					
	Reps					
	Weight					
	Reps					
	Weight					
	Reps					
	Weight					
	Reps					
	Weight					
	Reps					
	Weight					
	Reps					
	Weight					
	Reps					

CARDIO WORKOUT

Exercise	Duration	Pace	Heart Rate	Calories

Notes:

DAILY CALORIE TARGET:

BREAKFAST	Protein	Carbs	Fat	Fiber	Sodium	Calories

SNACK	Protein	Carbs	Fat	Fiber	Sodium	Calories

LUNCH	Protein	Carbs	Fat	Fiber	Sodium	Calories

SNACK	Protein	Carbs	Fat	Fiber	Sodium	Calories

DINNER	Protein	Carbs	Fat	Fiber	Sodium	Calories

SNACK	Protein	Carbs	Fat	Fiber	Sodium	Calories

	Protein	Carbs	Fat	Fiber	Sodium	Calories
DAILY TOTALS						
DAILY GOALS						
% DAILY GOALS	%	%	%	%	%	%

WATER 1 cup per circle
(1 cup = 8 ounces ~ 240ml)

○ ○ ○ ○ ○ ○ ○ ○ ○ ○ ○ ○ ○

DATE: **WEEK:** **WEIGHT:**

Warm Up/ Stretching

Duration:

Exercise		Set 1	Set 2	Set 3	Set 4	Set 5
	Weight					
	Reps					
	Weight					
	Reps					
	Weight					
	Reps					
	Weight					
	Reps					
	Weight					
	Reps					
	Weight					
	Reps					
	Weight					
	Reps					
	Weight					
	Reps					
	Weight					
	Reps					
	Weight					
	Reps					
	Weight					
	Reps					
	Weight					
	Reps					
	Weight					
	Reps					

CARDIO WORKOUT

Exercise	Duration	Pace	Heart Rate	Calories

Notes:

DAILY CALORIE TARGET: ☐

BREAKFAST	Protein	Carbs	Fat	Fiber	Sodium	Calories

SNACK	Protein	Carbs	Fat	Fiber	Sodium	Calories

LUNCH	Protein	Carbs	Fat	Fiber	Sodium	Calories

SNACK	Protein	Carbs	Fat	Fiber	Sodium	Calories

DINNER	Protein	Carbs	Fat	Fiber	Sodium	Calories

SNACK	Protein	Carbs	Fat	Fiber	Sodium	Calories

DAILY TOTALS						
DAILY GOALS						
% DAILY GOALS	%	%	%	%	%	%

WATER   1 cup per circle
(1 cup = 8 ounces ~ 240ml)   ○○○○○○○○○○○○

DATE: **WEEK:** **WEIGHT:**

Warm Up/ Stretching   **Duration:**

Exercise		Set 1	Set 2	Set 3	Set 4	Set 5
	Weight					
	Reps					
	Weight					
	Reps					
	Weight					
	Reps					
	Weight					
	Reps					
	Weight					
	Reps					
	Weight					
	Reps					
	Weight					
	Reps					
	Weight					
	Reps					
	Weight					
	Reps					
	Weight					
	Reps					
	Weight					
	Reps					
	Weight					
	Reps					

CARDIO WORKOUT

Exercise	Duration	Pace	Heart Rate	Calories

Notes:

DAILY CALORIE TARGET:

BREAKFAST	Protein	Carbs	Fat	Fiber	Sodium	Calories

SNACK	Protein	Carbs	Fat	Fiber	Sodium	Calories

LUNCH	Protein	Carbs	Fat	Fiber	Sodium	Calories

SNACK	Protein	Carbs	Fat	Fiber	Sodium	Calories

DINNER	Protein	Carbs	Fat	Fiber	Sodium	Calories

SNACK	Protein	Carbs	Fat	Fiber	Sodium	Calories

DAILY TOTALS						
DAILY GOALS						
% DAILY GOALS	%	%	%	%	%	%

WATER   1 cup per circle
(1 cup = 8 ounces ~ 240ml)   ○ ○ ○ ○ ○ ○ ○ ○ ○ ○ ○ ○

DATE: _____ **WEEK:** _____ **WEIGHT:** _____

Warm Up/ Stretching

Duration: _____

Exercise		Set 1	Set 2	Set 3	Set 4	Set 5
	Weight					
	Reps					
	Weight					
	Reps					
	Weight					
	Reps					
	Weight					
	Reps					
	Weight					
	Reps					
	Weight					
	Reps					
	Weight					
	Reps					
	Weight					
	Reps					
	Weight					
	Reps					
	Weight					
	Reps					
	Weight					
	Reps					
	Weight					
	Reps					
	Weight					
	Reps					

CARDIO WORKOUT

Exercise	Duration	Pace	Heart Rate	Calories

Notes:

DAILY CALORIE TARGET:

BREAKFAST	Protein	Carbs	Fat	Fiber	Sodium	Calories

SNACK	Protein	Carbs	Fat	Fiber	Sodium	Calories

LUNCH	Protein	Carbs	Fat	Fiber	Sodium	Calories

SNACK	Protein	Carbs	Fat	Fiber	Sodium	Calories

DINNER	Protein	Carbs	Fat	Fiber	Sodium	Calories

SNACK	Protein	Carbs	Fat	Fiber	Sodium	Calories
DAILY TOTALS						
DAILY GOALS						
% DAILY GOALS	%	%	%	%	%	%

WATER 1 cup per circle
(1 cup = 8 ounces ~ 240ml)

○○○○○○○○○○○○○○○

DATE:		WEEK:		WEIGHT:	

Warm Up/ Stretching				Duration:	

Exercise		Set 1	Set 2	Set 3	Set 4	Set 5
	Weight					
	Reps					
	Weight					
	Reps					
	Weight					
	Reps					
	Weight					
	Reps					
	Weight					
	Reps					
	Weight					
	Reps					
	Weight					
	Reps					
	Weight					
	Reps					
	Weight					
	Reps					
	Weight					
	Reps					
	Weight					
	Reps					
	Weight					
	Reps					
	Weight					
	Reps					

CARDIO WORKOUT

Exercise	Duration	Pace	Heart Rate	Calories

Notes:

DAILY CALORIE TARGET:

BREAKFAST	Protein	Carbs	Fat	Fiber	Sodium	Calories

SNACK	Protein	Carbs	Fat	Fiber	Sodium	Calories

LUNCH	Protein	Carbs	Fat	Fiber	Sodium	Calories

SNACK	Protein	Carbs	Fat	Fiber	Sodium	Calories

DINNER	Protein	Carbs	Fat	Fiber	Sodium	Calories

SNACK	Protein	Carbs	Fat	Fiber	Sodium	Calories

	Protein	Carbs	Fat	Fiber	Sodium	Calories
DAILY TOTALS						
DAILY GOALS						
% DAILY GOALS	%	%	%	%	%	%

WATER 1 cup per circle
(1 cup = 8 ounces ~ 240ml)   ○○○○○○○○○○○○

DATE: | **WEEK:** | **WEIGHT:**

Warm Up/ Stretching | **Duration:**

Exercise		Set 1	Set 2	Set 3	Set 4	Set 5
	Weight					
	Reps					
	Weight					
	Reps					
	Weight					
	Reps					
	Weight					
	Reps					
	Weight					
	Reps					
	Weight					
	Reps					
	Weight					
	Reps					
	Weight					
	Reps					
	Weight					
	Reps					
	Weight					
	Reps					
	Weight					
	Reps					
	Weight					
	Reps					
	Weight					
	Reps					

CARDIO WORKOUT

Exercise	Duration	Pace	Heart Rate	Calories

Notes:

DAILY CALORIE TARGET:

BREAKFAST	Protein	Carbs	Fat	Fiber	Sodium	Calories

SNACK	Protein	Carbs	Fat	Fiber	Sodium	Calories

LUNCH	Protein	Carbs	Fat	Fiber	Sodium	Calories

SNACK	Protein	Carbs	Fat	Fiber	Sodium	Calories

DINNER	Protein	Carbs	Fat	Fiber	Sodium	Calories

SNACK	Protein	Carbs	Fat	Fiber	Sodium	Calories

	Protein	Carbs	Fat	Fiber	Sodium	Calories
DAILY TOTALS						
DAILY GOALS						
% DAILY GOALS	%	%	%	%	%	%

WATER   1 cup per circle
(1 cup = 8 ounces ~ 240ml)   ○○○○○○○○○○○○○○○

DATE: **WEEK:** **WEIGHT:**

Warm Up/ Stretching **Duration:**

Exercise		Set 1	Set 2	Set 3	Set 4	Set 5
	Weight					
	Reps					
	Weight					
	Reps					
	Weight					
	Reps					
	Weight					
	Reps					
	Weight					
	Reps					
	Weight					
	Reps					
	Weight					
	Reps					
	Weight					
	Reps					
	Weight					
	Reps					
	Weight					
	Reps					
	Weight					
	Reps					
	Weight					
	Reps					

CARDIO WORKOUT

Exercise	Duration	Pace	Heart Rate	Calories

Notes:

DAILY CALORIE TARGET:

BREAKFAST	Protein	Carbs	Fat	Fiber	Sodium	Calories

SNACK	Protein	Carbs	Fat	Fiber	Sodium	Calories

LUNCH	Protein	Carbs	Fat	Fiber	Sodium	Calories

SNACK	Protein	Carbs	Fat	Fiber	Sodium	Calories

DINNER	Protein	Carbs	Fat	Fiber	Sodium	Calories

SNACK	Protein	Carbs	Fat	Fiber	Sodium	Calories

	Protein	Carbs	Fat	Fiber	Sodium	Calories
DAILY TOTALS						
DAILY GOALS						
% DAILY GOALS	%	%	%	%	%	%

WATER   1 cup per circle
(1 cup = 8 ounces ~ 240ml)   ○○○○○○○○○○○○

DATE: **WEEK:**   **WEIGHT:**

Warm Up/ Stretching   **Duration:**

Exercise		Set 1	Set 2	Set 3	Set 4	Set 5
	Weight					
	Reps					
	Weight					
	Reps					
	Weight					
	Reps					
	Weight					
	Reps					
	Weight					
	Reps					
	Weight					
	Reps					
	Weight					
	Reps					
	Weight					
	Reps					
	Weight					
	Reps					
	Weight					
	Reps					
	Weight					
	Reps					
	Weight					
	Reps					
	Weight					
	Reps					

CARDIO WORKOUT

Exercise	Duration	Pace	Heart Rate	Calories

Notes:

DAILY CALORIE TARGET:

BREAKFAST	Protein	Carbs	Fat	Fiber	Sodium	Calories

SNACK	Protein	Carbs	Fat	Fiber	Sodium	Calories

LUNCH	Protein	Carbs	Fat	Fiber	Sodium	Calories

SNACK	Protein	Carbs	Fat	Fiber	Sodium	Calories

DINNER	Protein	Carbs	Fat	Fiber	Sodium	Calories

SNACK	Protein	Carbs	Fat	Fiber	Sodium	Calories
DAILY TOTALS						
DAILY GOALS						
% DAILY GOALS	%	%	%	%	%	%

WATER   1 cup per circle
(1 cup = 8 ounces ~ 240ml)   ◯ ◯ ◯ ◯ ◯ ◯ ◯ ◯ ◯ ◯ ◯ ◯

DATE: **WEEK:** **WEIGHT:**

Warm Up/ Stretching **Duration:**

Exercise		Set 1	Set 2	Set 3	Set 4	Set 5
	Weight					
	Reps					
	Weight					
	Reps					
	Weight					
	Reps					
	Weight					
	Reps					
	Weight					
	Reps					
	Weight					
	Reps					
	Weight					
	Reps					
	Weight					
	Reps					
	Weight					
	Reps					
	Weight					
	Reps					
	Weight					
	Reps					
	Weight					
	Reps					

CARDIO WORKOUT

Exercise	Duration	Pace	Heart Rate	Calories

Notes:

DAILY CALORIE TARGET:

BREAKFAST	Protein	Carbs	Fat	Fiber	Sodium	Calories

SNACK	Protein	Carbs	Fat	Fiber	Sodium	Calories

LUNCH	Protein	Carbs	Fat	Fiber	Sodium	Calories

SNACK	Protein	Carbs	Fat	Fiber	Sodium	Calories

DINNER	Protein	Carbs	Fat	Fiber	Sodium	Calories

SNACK	Protein	Carbs	Fat	Fiber	Sodium	Calories

	Protein	Carbs	Fat	Fiber	Sodium	Calories
DAILY TOTALS						
DAILY GOALS						
% DAILY GOALS	%	%	%	%	%	%

WATER   1 cup per circle
(1 cup = 8 ounces ~ 240ml)   ○○○○○○○○○○○○

DATE:		WEEK:		WEIGHT:	

Warm Up/ Stretching			Duration:	

Exercise		Set 1	Set 2	Set 3	Set 4	Set 5
	Weight					
	Reps					
	Weight					
	Reps					
	Weight					
	Reps					
	Weight					
	Reps					
	Weight					
	Reps					
	Weight					
	Reps					
	Weight					
	Reps					
	Weight					
	Reps					
	Weight					
	Reps					
	Weight					
	Reps					
	Weight					
	Reps					
	Weight					
	Reps					

CARDIO WORKOUT

Exercise	Duration	Pace	Heart Rate	Calories

Notes:

DAILY CALORIE TARGET:

BREAKFAST	Protein	Carbs	Fat	Fiber	Sodium	Calories

SNACK	Protein	Carbs	Fat	Fiber	Sodium	Calories

LUNCH	Protein	Carbs	Fat	Fiber	Sodium	Calories

SNACK	Protein	Carbs	Fat	Fiber	Sodium	Calories

DINNER	Protein	Carbs	Fat	Fiber	Sodium	Calories

SNACK	Protein	Carbs	Fat	Fiber	Sodium	Calories

DAILY TOTALS						
DAILY GOALS						
% DAILY GOALS	%	%	%	%	%	%

WATER 1 cup per circle
(1 cup = 8 ounces ~ 240ml)   ○○○○○○○○○○○○

Manufactured by Amazon.ca
Acheson, AB

12300902R00068